Read & Re...

FOR
KS2

PAGE
1

Read & Respond

FOR KS2

Author: Sylvia Clements

Development Editor: Simret Brar

Editor: Tracy Kewley

Assistant Editor: Vicky Butt

Series Designer: Anna Oliwa

Designer: Q2A Media

Illustrations: Paul Howard

Text © 2008 Sylvia Clements © 2008 Scholastic Ltd

Designed using Adobe InDesign

Published by Scholastic Ltd, Villiers House,
Clarendon Avenue, Leamington Spa,
Warwickshire CV32 5PR
www.scholastic.co.uk

Printed by Bell & Bain
1 2 3 4 5 6 7 8 9   8 9 0 1 2 3 4 5 6 7

British Library Cataloguing-in-Publication Data
A catalogue record for this book is available from the British
Library.
ISBN 978-1407-10003-6

Acknowledgements

The publishers gratefully acknowledge permission to reproduce
the following copyright material: **Egmonts UK Ltd** for the use
of extracts and the book cover from *The Owl Who Was Afraid
of the Dark* by Jill Tomlinson. Text © 1968, The Estate of Jill
Tomlinson. Cover illustration © 2000, Paul Howard (Text 1968,
Methuen and Co Ltd; Cover 2000, Egmont UK Ltd, London).
Paul Howard for the use of illustrations from *The Owl Who Was
Afraid of the Dark* by Jill Tomlinson Illustrations © 2000, Paul
Howard (2000, Egmont Books Ltd.). Every effort has been made
to trace copyright holders for the works reproduced in this book,
and the publishers apologise for any inadvertent omissions.

About the book

The Owl Who Was Afraid of the Dark, first published in 1968, is a timeless story for young children, which deals with overcoming fear and growing up. Although on the surface a simple story, aimed at the very young, it has many sub plots which thread consistently through the book. It provides an excellent example of story structure which the children can use as a model for their own writing.

The theme of the dark is dealt with on multiple levels, with Jill Tomlinson building up clever images which complement the simplicity of the basic story, widening the appeal of the book to younger and older children.

It is a useful book for literacy lessons as the abridged, beautifully illustrated picture book version could be used with less confident learners alongside the longer story. An audio cassette of the book, complete and unabridged, read by Maureen Lipman, is also available and provides opportunities for even more flexible learning – groups can work on chapters with a cassette recorder for more intense study.

The book tracks how Plop overcomes his fear of the dark by increasing his knowledge about it through conversations with different characters he meets in the vicinity of his home. Eventually, after being convinced that the dark is 'super', and finally accepting who he is, a nocturnal barn owl, he leaves the nest to go hunting with his parents.

The humorous sub plots detail how Plop improves his landing skills and learns about his dietary preferences – leading up to his ability to fly the nest and hunt for his own food. The children may be able to relate their own areas of growth and development to those of Plop.

There are many opportunities for cross-curricular links, particularly in PHSE, science and art, as well as superb opportunities for really creative display work!

About the author

Jill Tomlinson trained as an opera singer but decided to have a family whilst her voice matured. Due to illness this chosen path could not be fulfilled. After embarking on a journalism course, she finally realised her ambition was to become a writer of children's stories. Despite rejection of her manuscripts, she eventually became a published author. Illness intervened and Jill Tomlinson had to rely on her family to carry out the research about young animals on her behalf, in response to her questions. Jill was diagnosed with multiple sclerosis and died at the young age of 45. Despite unimaginable physical difficulties, Jill Tomlinson's stories are brimming over with gentle humour and warm, heart-felt messages to young children everywhere.

Facts and figures
The Owl Who Was Afraid of the Dark
Author: Jill Tomlinsion
First published: 1968 by Methuen and Co Ltd.
Jill Tomlinson's books all use young animals in stories which reach out to meet the emotional needs of young children.

Guided reading

Introducing Plop

On opening the cover of this book, the reader comes face to face with a pleading pair of black eyes, set on a tilted head which is perched on a fluffy, rotund little body which in turn is perched upon a six line description of the owlet himself. Before even starting to read the book the reader is drawn to the main character, who we are told is 'just perfect except for ONE thing…' Ask the children what effect the capitals for the word 'ONE' have and why there an ellipsis. We are hooked! We want to read on!

Dark is exciting

The first chapter introduces us to Plop, who he lives with and where he lives. Ask the children what we learn about Plop from the initial piece of dialogue between Plop and his mother. (Plop is resolute and determined but also obedient he does as his mother asks.) What can they tell you about Mrs Barn Owl? (She is caring and thoughtful and wants to help her son to help himself.) Ask the children to identify the words in italics. Who speaks them and why are they shown in italics? (Mrs Barn Owl uses them for emphasis – to make a point.)

Plop is reluctant to leave the nest. What is he nervous about? (He is not an accomplished lander.) In each chapter Plop leaves the landing branch in the same manner. Ask the children why it is funny. (You expect him to try to fly from the branch but he falls instead.) In each chapter Plop's fall to earth surprises his target, who, not expecting to encounter a barn owl, understandably mistakes him for something else. Plop meets a boy who describes fireworks to Plop. How would the children describe fireworks to someone who hadn't seen them before? Plop uses capital letters in some of his dialogue. Why is this? (To re-enforce the fact that he still does not like the dark.) Why do they think Plop agreed to watch the fireworks? (He had his parents on either side of him and he was inquisitive.)

Dark is kind

The end of the fireworks signifies bedtime for the boy, but it is the time when Plop should be starting his 'day'. Plop is invited to go hunting with his father – an integral part of barn owl life – but he makes an excuse not to go. This occurs throughout the book until the end, when he surprises his father and changes his mind. Ask the children why Plop makes an excuse. How does his father react? Why do they think this is? (His father understands Plop's feelings and does not want to force him – he will wait for Plop until he is ready.)

Each night when Plop's father returns from hunting, there is humorous dialogue between Plop and his father. What do the children think it is about what is said that makes it funny? (Plop swallows his dinner and asks what it is *afterwards*. He speaks in short, direct sentences and innocently assumes that there is more to eat after eating a whole mouse!)

Ask the children to identify the behaviour patterns typical of nocturnal animals – they go to sleep when it gets light and are active all night. Plop, being a baby, had a midnight rest (as a child has an afternoon sleep).

In the section where Plop leaves the nest, ask the children to identify the sentence which appeared in Chapter 1. ('Actually, I'm a barn owl.') How does Plop land this time? Is he improving yet? The old lady tells Plop that dark hides things – why would the lady want to hide the fact that she is old? What does she do in the dark to make her feel better? This chapter contains humour but has sad, serious undertones. Can the children find the other adjectives the old lady uses to describe the dark? ('Quiet' and 'restful'.) Can the children find examples of humour (not a night bird, 'just an old bird') and contrast it with examples of sadness (it hides 'shabby furniture and the hole in the carpet' – we can assume that the elderly lady has little money to replace these things). What two lessons does she teach Plop about manners?

Guided reading

Dark is fun

Plop is again invited to go hunting and again he makes an excuse which his father patiently accepts. Plop's clumsiness and immaturity are reinforced by the descriptions of the adult barn owls in flight. What simile is used to describe Mr Barn Owl as he swoops off? ('Like a great, silent jet aeroplane'.) His mother also leaves to hunt, and her departure is also described using a simile – she floats off 'like a white feather'. When alone Plop repeats himself – why is this? (He is nervous and is trying to take his mind off the darkness.) Ask the children what they do if they are ever nervous. Plop is enticed to investigate the noises he hears. Is this a good idea – to go somewhere without your parents' knowledge?

Invite the children to locate the repeated line once again. How does Plop land this time? Why does the boy emphasise the word 'bonfire'? What is the difference between a bonfire and a campfire? Discuss the Scouts and Guides movement and whether any of the children have been camping. Why couldn't Plop be a Scout or a Cub? (He is too young and would look silly in a uniform. This seems ironic as barn owls don't actually talk let alone wear clothes – this is an example of the author setting her own boundaries between the fictional world and the real world.) What does Plop do that shows he is learning to be responsible? Plop's supper ends the chapter on a humorous note as his father's generous offering once again fails to satiate Plop's voracious appetite.

Dark is necessary

Half way through the story, Plop is slowly showing signs of becoming a night bird – he sleeps until well into the afternoon and his landing ability is improving slightly. We find further evidence of Plop's mischievous and humorous nature as he teases the squirrels that live in his tree. Why does his mother send him off to find out more about the dark? (She wants

some peace and quiet and knows it is pointless trying to get him to sleep.) His encounter with the young girl is slightly confrontational – both characters become defensive as the other asks probing questions. Can the children relate their understanding of Christmas to the class, imagining they were telling a child who had not heard of it? Through the course of their encounter girl and owl build up respect for each other and their discussion ends with an act of kindness. What is this and how do they both make up for their earlier insults?

Dark is fascinating

Plop's parents are both evidently very tired from their hunting expeditions and wish to get a good day's sleep. Which of his parents is the most understanding? How does his mother deal with his inability to sleep during the day? (She sends him off to find more information about the dark.) Plop's departure from the nest is different this time – how is it changing? Plop learns about bats and hedgehogs in this chapter. What facts does he learn? Plop feels very pleased with himself when he returns from meeting the Father Christmas lady and is full of confidence and extremely hungry! Why do the children think this is? (She drew a complimentary drawing of him and loved his screech – it boosted his self-image.)

Dark is wonderful

In 'Dark is wonderful', we are treated to a wonderful description of Plop's parents as they leave to hunt. The image created impresses upon the reader how majestic and ghostly these beautiful birds are. Plop has not attained this status yet but his landing is improving – he now lands with a soft bump as opposed to a thud! In this encounter, Plop learns about the star constellations and more humour is woven into the narrative as we are invited to picture Plop scuttling along the telescope as he listens to and questions his teacher. On returning home, having politely excused himself, Plop is obviously intrigued with his new-found knowledge – he is too busy relating the facts to eat, despite his hunger. The chapter also sees a further change in Plop – he spends the night describing the star constellations to his parents, who dutifully listen. Plop is growing accustomed to the dark without realising! Like a real night owl, he sleeps all through the daylight hours for the first time.

Dark is beautiful

In the final chapter Plop's encounter is somewhat different. How is this so? (He meets another animal rather than a human.) Although he falls off his branch he lands softly, providing further evidence of his development.

The animals develop an immediate bond – Plop is full of respect for the cat and the cat respects Plop's naivety. Before leaving to explore the night, Plop responsibly tells his mother where he is going. This action maintains the consistency of character development. Orion shows Plop the wonders of the night and describes all the different nights in an enchanting, enticing way. Plop is finally convinced.

The story is beautifully concluded by Plop summing up everything he has learned from all the characters and then providing his own opinion. This is followed humorously by the 'feeding' dialogue between Plop and his father, but instead of making an excuse as in all the previous chapters, Plop agrees to go hunting with his father. The emphasis on 'long' demonstrates that although Plop is now a fully fledged night bird, he is still young because his appreciation of time is different to that of an adult's. Draw the children's attention to the last 'sentence'. Why is it not actually a sentence? (It does not have a verb.) It is a statement of fact – short and very effective. The illustration of the owls silhouetted against the moon complements the ending perfectly.

Shared reading

Extract 1

● This extract is the opening the book. Plop, the main character, is introduced with a description of his physical features – and the principal aspect of his personality, his fear of the dark, is revealed through the dialogue between himself and his mother.

● Invite the children to highlight the adjectives that describe Plop. What do they think the author means by 'knackety'? Is this a real word? Do they think it is effective? Why? (The use of alliteration helps the phrase to roll off the tongue. It is memorable because it is made up and creates a comical image.)

● Highlight the words in italics. Who are they spoken by? (Plop's mother.) Why are they used? (To emphasise that Plop is a night bird.)

● We can deduce that Plop is stubborn. What evidence is there for this? Why have capital letters been used for 'AT ALL'?

Extract 2

● In this extract, the descriptions of adult barn owls in flight – evoking powerful, peaceful images – are contrasted by the comical dialogue and descriptions of Plop as he 'leaves' the nest to discover more about the dark.

● Read the first two sentences. Ask the children to tell you which words make this a powerful description? ('Great', 'white', 'drift', 'melt'.) What effect do the words have? (The owls seem to be a part of the night; calm and peaceful.)

● What do the children understand by 'pricked all over with tiny stars'? (The sky is like a covering or blanket and the stars seem to be holes letting in light.)

● How does this extract change from being serious to humorous? (Through the introduction of dialogue.)

● How does the author describe Plop's landing in this extract? Compare this with his landing in Chapter 2. How does it differ?

Extract 3

● Here the story concludes. Plop details what each character thought of the dark before proclaiming that he now thinks 'DARK IS SUPER'. Why do the children think the author used capitals? (For emphasis and clarity.)

● Why does Plop not want his father to know his feelings? (He wants to surprise him.) How does he let his father know he is no longer afraid? (He agrees to go hunting instead of making an excuse.) The word 'long' is in italics – why? (The time elapsed since Plop overcame his fear feels long to him as he is so young.)

● Why do the children think that Plop is in the middle of his parents as they leave to go hunting? (Despite no longer being afraid, it is his first trip, and still very young and in need of protection.)

● Draw attention to the last sentence – a good example of how very brief words can be more punchy and effective than long, complex sentences.

Extract 1

Dark is exciting

Plop was a baby barn owl, and he lived with his mummy and daddy at the top of a very tall tree in a field.

Plop was fat and fluffy.

He had a beautiful heart-shaped ruff.

He had enormous, round eyes.

He had very knackety knees.

In fact he was exactly the same as every baby barn owl that has ever been – except for one thing.

Plop was afraid of the dark.

'You *can't* be afraid of the dark,' said his mummy. 'Owls are *never* afraid of the dark.'

'This one is,' Plop said.

'But owls are *night* birds,' she said.

Plop looked down at his toes. 'I don't want to be a night bird,' he mumbled. 'I want to be a day bird.'

'You *are* what you *are*,' said Mrs Barn Owl firmly.

'Yes, I know,' agreed Plop, 'and what I are is afraid of the dark.'

'Oh dear,' said Mrs Barn Owl. It was clear that she was going to need a lot of patience. She shut her eyes and tried to think how best she could help Plop not to be afraid. Plop waited.

His mother opened her eyes again. 'Plop, you are only afraid of the dark because you don't know about it. What *do* you know about the dark?'

'It's black,' said Plop.

'Well that's wrong for a start. It can be silver or blue or grey or lots of other colours, but almost never black. What else do you know about it?'

'I don't like it,' said Plop. 'I do not like it AT ALL.'

'That's not *knowing* something,' said his mother. 'That's *feeling* something. I don't think you know anything about the dark at all.'

'Dark is nasty,' Plop said loudly.

Extract 2

Dark is wonderful

Plop's parents took off together side by side, their great white wings almost touching. Plop sat outside the nest-hole and watched them drift away into the darkness until they melted into each other and then disappeared altogether. It took quite a long time, because the stars were coming out and Plop could see a long way by their light and his owl's eyes.

He remembered what his mother had said about dark never being black. It certainly was not black tonight. It was more of a misty grey, and the sky was pricked all over with tiny stars.

'Drat!' said a voice from somewhere below Plop.

Plop started and peered down through the leaves. There was a man with some sort of contraption set up in front of him, standing there scowling up at the cloud which had hidden the moon. What was he doing?

Plop shut his eyes and took a deep breath, and fell off his branch.

He shot through the air like a white streak and landed with a soft bump.

'Heavens!' cried the man. 'A shooting star!'

'Actually I'm a barn owl,' said the shooting star. 'What's that thing you've got there?'

'A telescope,' said the man.

Text © 1968, The Estate of Jill Tomlinson; Illustrations © 2000, Paul Howard.

Extract 3

Dark is beautiful

'Well?' said his mother.

Plop took a deep breath. 'The small boy said DARK IS EXCITING. The old lady said DARK IS KIND. The Boy Scout said DARK IS FUN. The little girl said DARK IS NECESSARY. The Father Christmas Lady said DARK IS FASCINATING. The man with the telescope said DARK IS WONDERFUL and Orion the black cat says DARK IS BEAUTIFUL.'

'And what do you think, Plop?'

Plop looked up at his mother with twinkling eyes. 'I think,' he said. 'I think – DARK IS SUPER! But sssh! Daddy's coming. Don't say anything.'

Mr Barn Owl came in with a great flapping of wings. He dropped something at Plop's feet.

Plop swallowed it in one gulp. 'That was nice,' he said. 'What was it?'

'A vole.'

'I like vole,' said Plop. 'What's next?'

'Why don't you come with me and find out?' said Mr Barn Owl.

'Yes, please,' said Plop.

Mr Barn Owl blinked. 'What did you say?'

'I said "yes please",' Plop said. 'I would like to come hunting with you.'

'I thought you were afraid of the dark!'

'Me?' said Plop. 'Afraid of the dark! That was a *long* time ago!'

'Well!' said his father. 'What are we waiting for? A-hunting we will go!'

'Hey wait for me,' said Plop's mother. 'I'm coming too.'

So they took off together in the moonlight, Mr and Mrs Barn Owl on each side and Plop in the middle.

Plop – the night bird.

Text © 1968, The Estate of Jill Tomlinson; Illustrations © 2000, Paul Howard.

Plot, character and setting

Plop ~ the day bird

> **Objective:** To identify how characters are built up from small details.
> **What you need:** Copies of *The Owl Who Was Afraid of the Dark,* photocopiable page 15, writing materials.

What to do

● Explain that characters are made up of two elements – physical appearance, which we learn about through descriptive details, and personality, which is inferred from a character's actions and dialogue. Read Chapter 1 with the children, asking them to listen out for details about Plop's character.

● Record the children's contributions on a whiteboard in one of two columns – one for personality and one for appearance.

● Make a list of general personality traits such as friendly, shy, obedient, funny, and so on. Ask the children to tell you what they think Plop is like. Can they substantiate this? Demonstrate how to find evidence in the text to support points of view. For example, you could say that Plop is responsible because when Orion asks him to go hunting he goes to tell his mother where he is going first. Show the children how to locate and describe the evidence for this.

> **Differentiation**
> **For older/more confident learners:** Ask the children to find the evidence to support the character traits on photocopiable page 15. Encourage them to suggest extra traits and substantiate these with evidence.
> **For younger/less confident learners:** Provide the evidence for each personality trait and ask the children to match the trait to the evidence.

Mr and Mrs Barn Owl

> **Objective:** To investigate how figurative language is used and to consider the use of similes, metaphors and powerful verbs.
> **What you need:** Copies of *The Owl Who Was Afraid of the Dark,* writing materials, photographs/video clips of barn owls, word processing package.

What to do

● Plop is a fluffy, awkward, humorous little bird – characteristics which are emphasised by the contrast between Plop and his parents who are grand, elegant, majestic birds. In order to create the image of the parents, the author uses a number of similes and metaphors to describe how they stand ('drawn up as still as carvings') and how they fly ('like a great white moth', 'like a great silent jet aeroplane', 'like a white feather'). She also describes their flight using powerful verbs ('floated', 'swooped', 'drifted', 'melted', 'circled').

● Ask the children to locate the similes and metaphors which describe the adult barn owls. Type these up and print them for use as labels.

● Show photographs of barn owls and clips of barn owls in flight. (Search the internet for images.) Discuss features, such as the beak, talons, feathers, wings, eyes.

● Encourage the children to create their own similes and metaphors to describe the adult barn owls.

● Print the children's work and display it around the barn owls images.

> **Differentiation**
> **For older/more confident learners:** Encourage the children to write a descriptive paragraph using their own similes and metaphors to describe the take off, flight and hunting activities of an adult barn owl. Encourage the use of powerful verbs.
> **For younger/less confident learners:** Provide similes and metaphors and allow the children to match them to the correct physical feature, for example 'His eyes were like shiny black marbles.'

Plot, character and setting

Plop's world

Objective: To look at how descriptive language is used to build up details of settings.
What you need: Copies of *The Owl Who Was Afraid of the Dark,* Photocopiable page 16, drawing and writing materials.

What to do

● This is an ongoing activity.
● Explain that we can build up a picture of the story setting in our minds through the detail provided in the text. Ask the children to listen out for details about where Plop lives.
● Mount a large piece of paper near to the area where the children listen to the story. After each session, add any setting details – preferably as drawings but words will suffice.
● The first detail will be the large tree in a field with a landing branch and nest-hole being evident. This is the focal point of the story, where Plop returns to discuss his feelings with his parents. As the story progresses, details will be added around the tree, such as the woods, the log, the garden with the swing and so on.
● Ask the children to complete photocopiable page 16 independently.

Differentiation
For older/more confident learners: Invite the children to write short descriptions of the various features to enhance the setting descriptions in the book. For example, they can describe the type of tree, how its branches spread, what other creatures live amongst its branches and in its trunk.
For younger/less confident learners: Provide the children with copies of the pages where the settings are described and invite them to highlight the words which describe the setting.

Moonlit nights

Objective: Explore how texts appeal to readers using descriptive language.
What you need: Copies of *The Owl Who Was Afraid of the Dark,* writing materials.

What to do

● This activity should be completed after reading the final chapter.
● Plop finally realises that he is no longer afraid of the dark after meeting Orion. Why do the children think that it was Orion who was able to convince Plop that he was a night bird after all? (He was an animal and partially 'nocturnal' too – they had more in common.)
● Orion's descriptions of different types of nights convince Plop that there is much to be enjoyed and discovered. Ask the children to scan through Chapter 7 in groups to find all these descriptions and record them on whiteboards. Discuss which descriptions the children like best and why.

● Orion states that moonlight is magic and turns everything to silver. Read the poem 'Silver' by Walter de la Mare.
● Work together to create additional descriptions of different types of nights. Think about how different sorts of weather and the seasons would affect the night and the locations, such as city or country. What can they hear? What else do they think Orion would have to show Plop if they were to go hunting together?

Differentiation
For older/more confident learners: Imagine Plop went hunting with Orion instead of going back to the nest-hole. Think about what they may have seen and write a description of what Plop may have told his parents about his trip when he returned home.
For younger/less confident learners: Discuss children's own experiences of the dark and encourage them to create a sentence to describe what the dark was like.

Plot, character and setting

Plop's plot

Objective: To know that narratives use a beginning, middle and end in which events are sequenced logically and conflicts resolved.
What you need: Copies of *The Owl Who Was Afraid of the Dark,* photocopiable page 17, writing materials.

What to do

● Explain that narrative writing uses a beginning, middle and end and often involves the resolution of a conflict. Ask the children what the conflict is in this story? (Plop's fear of the dark.) Can they identify other minor conflicts which get resolved by the end of the story? (Plop learns how to fly and land and what he likes to eat.)
● Invite the children to imagine that they are Jill Tomlinson and that she has not yet written the book. Explain that writers will write a plot plan before they start their story to ensure that they know where the story is 'going'.
● Using photocopiable page 17, invite the children to fill in details of the plot by listing who Plop met, how each character described the dark and their reasoning for this. The children will need to refer to the text.

Differentiation
For older/more confident learners: Invite the children to create an additional character for Plop to meet. Decide what they think about the dark and what their reasoning is for this, for example, a cat burglar or a night watchman.
For younger/less confident learners: Read the relevant section of each chapter to the children as they are completing the table. Then ask for a summary of the main point of what they have heard.

Mistaken identity

Objective: To understand how dialogue is used and to identify the words spoken.
What you need: Copies of *The Owl Who Was Afraid of the Dark,* photocopiable page 18, writing materials.

What to do

● Recap the main plot – Plop leaves the nest-hole to meet characters who enlighten him about the virtues of darkness. Invite the children to identify the other threads which run through the story – Plop encounters a range of dietary treats, he improves his landing skills and he is the subject of mistaken identity.
● Each mistaken identity occurs as Plop leaves the landing branch in order to go and meet a new character. The author uses the mistaken identity as a means of establishing dialogue between the two characters.
● Ask the children why they think the six humans mistook him for something other than a barn owl whereas the cat knew what he was immediately? (Both were 'night animals'; Plop arrived at night, so his arrival was expected.)
● Photocopiable page 18 lists the characters Plop meets. Discuss how speech marks enclose actual words that are spoken by characters. Then invite the children to complete the boxes with the words spoken by the characters when they first see Plop, for example, 'Ooh! A giant Catherine-Wheel!'.
● Discuss the use of exclamation marks to show the characters' surprise.

Differentiation
For older/more confident learners: Ask the children to draw Plop and Orion with a speech bubble for each picture. Invite them to find the dialogue between the characters and to insert this into the speech bubbles.
For younger/less confident learners: Copy out the relevant sentence from the book for each character and invite the children to use a highlighter pen to highlight the spoken words. They can then transfer these into the speech bubbles on the photocopiable sheet.

Plot, character and setting

Food glorious food!

> **Objective:** To present events and characters through dialogue to engage the interest of an audience. To look at how dialogue is presented in narrative and how it is written in a play script.
> **What you need:** Copies of Chapter 4 (first two pages), writing materials.

What to do

● One of Plop's characteristics is his love of food and his willingness to try anything new! Explain that we learn this through reading the dialogue between Plop and his parents. The first part of Chapter 4 'Dark is necessary' provides evidence for this. It also demonstrates the humorous side of the story.

● Provide the children with copies of the first two pages of Chapter 4. Invite them to highlight the words spoken by Plop, Mr Barn Owl and Mrs Barn Owl. In a play these would be read by actors taking on the character roles. Explain that all the other words are the narrative. In a play these would be read by a narrator.

● Demonstrate how to write up the spoken words in the form of a playscript. Write any directions, for example how the words are spoken or what actions are carried out, in brackets by the script.

● Choose children to take on the roles of Plop and Mr and Mrs Barn Owl then act out the scene with a narrator.

> **Differentiation**
> **For older/more confident learners:** Groups of the children could choose a further section of the book where there is considerable dialogue and translate it into a playscript and perform it to the class.
> **For younger/less confident learners:** Work in a group and hand the children strips of paper with the words on, numbered in sequential order.

Take a closer look

> **Objective:** To identify and make notes of the main points of sections of text.
> **What you need:** Copies of Chapter 6, writing materials, large sheet of blank paper for each group.

What to do

● After reading Chapter 6 'Dark is wonderful', ask the children to detail the main points Plop learns from the man with the telescope. Record the suggestions on the board in the form of a spidergram (a circle with 'Dark is wonderful' in the centre and lines off for each point identified.)

● The children can then work in groups, with the text in front of them, to identify all the things which Plop learned about the stars.

● Summarise the points as a list of bullet point facts, for example:

● a telescope is for looking at stars and planets
● a meteor is a shooting star
● Sirius is the Dog Star and is fifty-four million, million miles away
● the Pole Star is directly over the North Pole.

● The children could then word process the facts.

> **Differentiation**
> **For older/more confident learners:** The children could carry out a similar exercise for Chapter 4, producing a list of 'facts' about Father Christmas.
> **For younger/less confident learners:** Read small sections of the text and invite the children to relate back any facts they have learned, with the LSA recording their suggestions on the spidergram.

Plop – The day bird

Plop's *physical* characteristics are detailed in the Introduction and in Chapter 1.
Use the descriptions to label this diagram of Plop.

We learn about a character's personality from their actions and words. Use
Chapter 1 to list some of Plop's personality traits and back these up with
supporting evidence from the text.

Personality trait	Supporting evidence	Page and line number
Stubborn		
Obedient		
Inquisitive		
Polite		
Responsible		

Illustration © 2000, Paul Howard.

Plot, character and setting

Plop's world

We can build up a picture of where Plop lives through the words which describe the story setting. The 'word picture' below has been created from all the information in the book that describes the story setting.

- As you read the book, record the page number where each setting feature is found.
- Use the word picture to draw your own illustration of Plop's world on a separate sheet.

Setting	Page number
Woods	
Log	
Campfire	
Garden with swing	
Bonfire at the end of the garden	
Sleeping town – houses with chimney pots near the church far from home	
Field	
Very tall tree	
…with landing branch	
…and nest-hole	
Dry leaves beneath the big tree	
Garden with deckchair	

Plot, character and setting

Plop's plot

Before starting to write, an author will plan the plot. Imagine you are Jill Tomlinson before she wrote the story. Complete the plot planner below to use as a framework for *The Owl Who Was Afraid of the Dark*.

PLOT SUMMARY

1. Plop is a baby barn owl who is afraid of the dark.
2. As the story progresses, he learns to accept the dark. This is due to meeting and talking to other people/animals about their opinions of the dark.
3. Meanwhile, his ability to land and fly improves.
4. He also discovers lots of new foods and learns about the diet of a barn owl.

Chapter	Who does Plop meet?	How do they describe the dark?	What is their reasoning for this?
1	Little boy	Dark is exciting	Because in the dark you can watch beautiful fireworks and have a bonfire.
2			
3			
4			
5			
6			

Mistaken identity

- Each time Plop leaves the security of his nest-hole to go out and discover more about the dark, he is mistaken for something other than a barn owl.
- Complete the boxes with the ACTUAL words the character uses when they first meet Plop.

The boy	The old lady

The boy scout	The little girl

The Father Christmas lady	The telescope man

Illustration © 2000, Paul Howard.

Talk about it

Dark is scary!

> **Objective:** To use group discussion to reflect on feelings and fears.
> **What you need:** A soft teddy bear, large sheets of sugar paper and marker pens.
> **Cross-curricular links:** PSHE.

What to do

● Sit in a circle. If the class is new to circle time, establish a clear set of circle time rules. Establish that if they want to speak they must be holding the bear. Everyone else should listen to the speaker. Explain that everything said in the circle is to stay in that setting. Ensure that the children do not feel pressurised to contribute and may pass.

● Discuss Plop's fear. What was his mother's reaction? (His fear was due to lack of knowledge – if he found out more he would

probably not be frightened.) Do they think this is good advice?

● Explain that lots of people are frightened of something or of certain situations and that it is fine to be frightened. Throw the teddy between the children and collate a list of common fears (heights, water, spiders and so on). Record these on the sugar paper – one per sheet.

● Take each example and invite the children to suggest why people may hold this fear. Record their suggestions on the sheets.

● Talk about how Plop overcame his fear and discuss how people could overcome their fears. Record suggestions on the sugar paper.

● Pass the bear around the circle allowing the children to say what they are frightened of – this should obviously be dealt with sensitively and you should ensure there is no-one who will use contributions to tease other children.

Excuses, excuses

> **Objective:** To use the language of possibility to investigate and reflect on the behaviour of a character and how this relates to their own lives.
> **What you need:** Copies of *The Owl Who Was Afraid of the Dark*, whiteboards and pens.
> **Cross-curricular links:** PHSE.

What to do

● Each night when Mr or Mrs Barn Owl went hunting, Plop declined their invitation to join them. Due to his fear of the dark, he made an excuse not to go. Discuss the difference between good/valid excuses and poor excuses.

● Divide the class into groups. Provide each group with copies of the book and give the group

scribe a whiteboard and pen. Ask the groups to scan through the book to find the three excuses Plop gave for not going hunting. Were the excuses good or bad? Did Plop's father accept the excuse? Why do they think this was the case? (He did because he knew the real reason Plop didn't want to go and respected his son's fear.)

> **Differentiation**
> **For older/more confident learners:** Allocate a more able/older child to each group to act as discussion leaders and scribes.
> **For younger/less confident learners:** 'Buddy' children with a more able child who is responsible for listening to their contribution and then relating it to the group as a whole on the child's behalf.

Talk about it

Plop the play

> **Objective:** To present a section of the story through dialogue to engage the interests of an audience.
> **What you need:** Photocopies of chosen sections of the text, highlighter pens.
> **Cross-curricular links:** Drama

What to do

● Choose a piece of dialogue from the book and write it on the board or display it on a whiteboard. Invite the children to identify and highlight the actual words spoken.

● Discuss films the children may have seen which have been adapted from books (for example *Peter Pan, Charlotte's Web*). Explain that films are created from scripts of the words spoken by characters and that the visual scenery and the actors' actions portray the rest of the narrative.

● Demonstrate how to create a piece of script from a section of the book. Invite the children to take on the roles of the characters involved. Explain that words in brackets and italics explain how to say the words, for example patiently, loudly.

● Divide the children into groups and allocate a photocopy of a section you wish them to write as a play. Encourage the children to highlight the words spoken (one colour for each character) and use this to act out the scene. Allow time to practise and then perform in front of the rest of the class.

> **Differentiation**
> **For older/more confident learners:** Ask the children to write out the section as a playscript with the characters' names in the margin and how the words are to be spoken and any actions in brackets and italics.
> **For younger/less confident learners:** Let the children work in a group with an LSA who will highlight the words on the photocopied sheet, then write the words out on a large sheet of paper. The children can then practise acting out, with the LSA. prompting.

Persuading plop ~ 1

> **Objective:** To establish a point of view through group discussion.
> **What you need:** Photocopiable page 22 (enlarged onto A3), writing materials.
> **Cross-curricular links:** Drama

What to do

● Recap the list of characters Plop met when investigating the dark, what their thoughts were about the dark and the reasons for their opinions. Explain what is meant by an opinion.

● Discuss other people who are very familiar with the dark through work or other activities – astronaut, cat burglar, security guard, lighthouse keeper, wizard. Talk about what these people do, what they may see, hear, feel.

● Split the class into groups and allocate a different character to each group. The group should imagine that they are the character and they meet Plop beneath the landing branch. They should decide which adjective best represents their character's opinion of the dark, for example 'calm', 'soothing' or 'magical'. They should then discuss and agree on their reasoning. The groups can use the photocopiable sheet to record their ideas.

> **Differentiation**
> **For older/more confident learners:** The children could write a dialogue between the new character and Plop which could then be performed.
> **For younger/less confident learners:** Put children together with an LSA who can lead the discussion and ask open questions to help guide the groups' pattern of thought, for example *What would a lighthouse keeper hear at night? What do you think he/she could see from the top of the lighthouse in the dark? What do you think the sea would be like in a storm?*

Talk about it

Persuading Plop ~ 2

Objectives: To follow up other's points of view; to show agreement or disagreement in whole-class discussion; to actively include and respond to all members of the group; to use drama strategies to explore issues.
What you need: Completed photocopiable page 22, a 'hot-seat', photocopiable page 23.
Cross-curricular links: Drama.

What to do

● The children should nominate one member of their group to go on the hot seat and be interviewed by the rest of the class, who are representing Plop. Then allocate the characters that are going to present a case to Plop.

● Before the hot seating takes place, each group prepares their own case from their completed photocopiable page 22 and also prepares some questions to ask the other characters. Provide guidance about how to ask open questions and help the children to think in new directions.

● When ready, the first character can take the hot seat. Ensure everyone gets into role as either Plop (the class) or the new character. The character begins by stating who he/she is and what they think of the dark. They can then take questions from the Plops in the audience!

● After the hot seat activity the children can complete photocopiable page 23. The results can be collated and the class can decide who the most persuasive character was.

Differentiation
For older/more confident learners: Children may take on the active roles or carry out the written work on behalf of the group.
For younger/less confident learners: 'Buddy' less confident learners with more confident learners and ensure that they are encouraged to make a contribution by asking questions and voicing their own opinion after the hot seating activity.

Images of the moon

Objective: To create poems and prepare them for performance, identifying appropriate tone, expression, volume and use of voices and other sounds.
What you need: Photocopiable page 24, writing materials, thesaurus.
Cross-curricular links: Art, drama.

What to do

● Invite the children to study the illustration of Plop and Orion sitting on the rooftops, staring out at the night. Draw attention to the moon. Have the children ever looked at the moon? Discuss how the moon changes.

● Ask the children to choose a verb to describe what the moon does such as 'shines'. Explain how to use a thesaurus to expand and improve upon the verb chosen.

● Recap what a simile is. Now ask what the moon looks like that is shiny for example 'pearly white teeth'. Put these together to form the first line of the poem: 'The moon gleams like a pearly white smile.'

● Brainstorm to extend the list of powerful verbs and objects which the moon resembles.

● The children should then collate their lists of similes – three similes to a verse. The poems can be set out as shown on photocopiable page 24. They can then perform their poems to the class.

Differentiation
For older/more confident learners: Allow the children to assimilate their own lists of verbs and similes. The children could also use metaphors and create an additional/alternative poem.
For younger/less confident learners: Using photocopiable page 24, invite the children to choose a verb and match it to an appropriate noun phrase to create their poem. They could write a collaborative poem and then perform it together.

Talk about it

Persuading Plop

Decide on a new character who will help to persuade Plop that the dark is not nasty. Complete the Mind Map with the character details, the adjective the character uses to describe the dark and the reasons why they think this. You are trying to change how Plop feels so make sure that your descriptions are really persuasive.

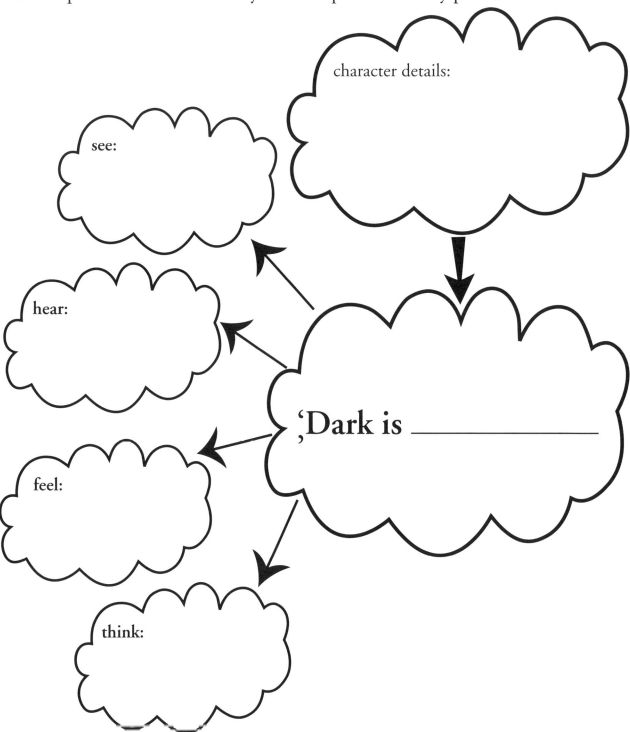

character details:

see:

hear:

feel:

think:

'Dark is _____

READ & RESPOND: Activities based on The Owl Who Was Afraid of the Dark

Plop's decision chart

Record each character's point of view about the dark. You can include the characters from the book and those created by your class. Record the main points each one made in the chart below. Now imagine you are Plop and tick the box which describes how much you agree or disagree with each point of view.

Character	Dark is…	Agree strongly	Agree	Disagree	Disagree strongly

Illustration © 2000, Paul Howard.

SECTION 5

Images of the moon

Complete the poem by choosing a verb from the list below to describe what the moon does. Then describe how it does this by comparing it to another object – you can choose from the list or create your own ideas.

The moon
    gleams
Like a polished smile,
    floats
Like a _____

_____

Like a _____

The moon

_____

Like a _____

_____

Like a _____

_____

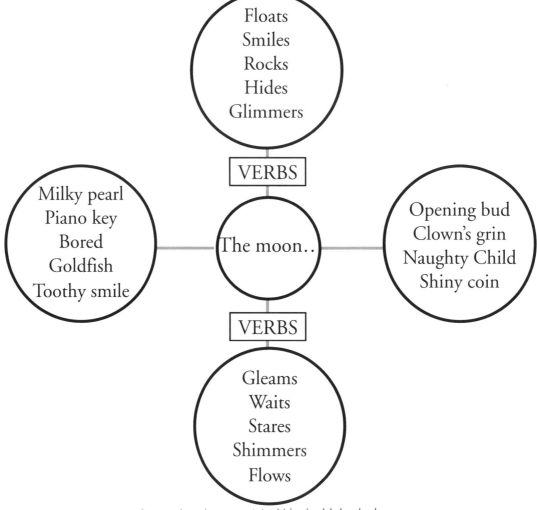

Floats
Smiles
Rocks
Hides
Glimmers

VERBS

Milky pearl
Piano key
Bored
Goldfish
Toothy smile

The moon..

Opening bud
Clown's grin
Naughty Child
Shiny coin

VERBS

Gleams
Waits
Stares
Shimmers
Flows

Activity based on an original idea by Moira Andrew.

Get writing

The Duck Who Was Afraid of the Water

> **Objective:** To plan a plot sequence for their own story.
> **What you need:** Photocopiable page 28, writing materials.

What to do
● Ask the children to recap the plot outline for *The Owl Who Was Afraid of the Dark* – he left the nest to discover more about the dark to help him overcome his fear, he learned to land as the story progressed, he learned about different foods and he was the subject of mistaken identity. Use this plot outline to plan a version of the story based upon a duck who was afraid of water.
● List what they would need to do to plan the story. What is the duckling called? What does he look like? Where does he live? Why is he different to the other ducklings in his family?

● Brainstorm a list of characters for the duck to meet. What will they say about water? Why do they think this? Who finally convinces the duck not to be afraid? How do they achieve this?
● Decide whether there are to be any sub-plots and if so what they will be.
● Complete the plot planner provided on photocopiable page 28.

> **Differentiation**
> **For older/more confident learners:** The children can decide on their own story focus and create their story planning sheet independently. Demonstrate how to create a mind map to record and extend ideas.
> **For younger/less confident learners:** The children can work in a group and the LSA can act as scribe, completing one enlarged A3 photocopiable – helping to develop the children's ideas through open questioning.

Barn owl fact file

> **Objectives:** To write a non-fiction report, grouping related material into paragraphs; to present the information using layout, format graphics and illustrations.
> **What you need:** Access to the internet, access to books about birds and owls, word processing package.

What to do
● Plop did not want to be a night bird. Ask the children if they would like to help Plop discover more about who he is. Explain that the task is to create a fact file about barn owls for Plop.
● Brainstorm what information the fact file may include, such as where barn owls live, what they eat and information about their flight. Enlarge photocopiable page 29 and complete one copy to use as a planner whilst researching on the internet. The Barn Owl Trust has a

wealth of information suitable for children at www.barnowltrust.org.uk.
● Invite the children to carry out research and then assimilate what they have found out into a number of key facts. Invite the children to report back to the class and complete the rest of the enlarged photocopiable page.
● Collate the facts that have been found as a class, demonstrating how to sort the information into paragraphs using headings, sub-headings, bullet points and other organisational features. Present the information as a fact file and publish.

> **Differentiation**
> **For older/more confident learners:** The children can create their own fact file. They may like to research several aspects of barn owl life and can complete the photocopiable page independently.
> **For younger/less confident learners:** Provide a list of specific questions for the children to answer from a pre-selected web page.

Get writing

Plop goes hunting

Objective: To compose sentences using adjectives, verbs and nouns for precision, clarity and impact.
What you need: Internet access, writing materials.

What to do

● After completing the story, the children could write a descriptive paragraph about Plop's first hunting expedition. Revisit the more 'serious' descriptions of Plop's parents. List them on the board. Show the children images and video clips of barn owls hunting and read factual descriptions of how barn owls hunt.

● Brainstorm vocabulary to describe the owls as they search for prey. What do they resemble? What effect do they have on the countryside scenery? Discuss the setting in terms of location and what can be heard and seen.

● Invite the children to suggest strong verbs to portray how the owls are flying before they identify prey, when prey is spotted and how they attack.

● Finally, once the owls have killed their prey, discuss how Plop now feels about the dark as he returns to the nest-hole. Impress upon the children the change in tempo through this piece of writing – a calm steady beginning and ending with tension building to a peak as the owls kill their prey.

● Once the brainstorming session is over and a wide range of ideas are listed on the board, the children can an introductory paragraph for a new chapter. Decide on its title (For example: Dark is exhilarating.)

Differentiation
For older/more confident learners: The children can use a thesaurus to expand their vocabulary choices. Encourage the use of a mixture of complex sentences and short simple sentences for impact.
For younger/less confident learners: Let the children work in a group with the teacher or LSA as scribe. Encourage suggestions by building the scene and then asking open questions. Record child ideas and encourage them to improve on their work until they are happy with the results.

I AM a night bird!

Objective: To write a piece of narrative text incorporating dialogue and descriptive elements.
What you need: Copies of *The Owl Who Was Afraid of the Dark,* writing materials, whiteboards.

What to do

● Read the last few pages of the book. Ask the children to imagine that when Plop exclaims that 'Dark is super!' his mother asks him what made him change his mind. What would Plop reply?

● Recall all the special things about the dark that the characters described to Plop. Invite the children to discuss their ideas in pairs, record them on whiteboards then hold them up. Collate the ideas on the board. Encourage the children to create descriptive noun phrases rather than just a list of ideas. Instead of 'You can watch fireworks in the dark.' Encourage the children to refer to the book to see how the fireworks were described, for example 'You can watch fireworks explode into a fountain of dancing stars.'

● Invite the children to write a piece dialogue between Plop and his mother. Demonstrate how to set out the dialogue. Start them off by writing up: Plop's mother smiled, a motherly sort of smile, 'What made you change your mind Plop?'

Differentiation
For older/more confident learners: Work with more confident learners to extend their vocabulary choices, develop complex sentences and use a thesaurus.
For younger/less confident learners: Encourage the children to build individual sentences beginning, 'I like the dark because…'

Get writing

Writing a review

Objective: To write a review of the book reflecting personal opinion and identifying features used to provoke reader reactions.
What you need: Copies of photocopiable page 30, writing materials, copies of *The Owl Who Was Afraid of the Dark*.

What to do

● After completing the book, invite the children to review the book to assist in their development of reading choices. Discuss the author, illustrations, the plot, character development, the style of the book, the messages it portrayed, favourite parts of the story and how they would improve it. They should consider who they feel would enjoy the book.
● After the whole-class discussion, ask the children to complete photocopiable page 30 individually. At the end of their review, they can give a score out of ten for the book.

● When the whole class has completed their reviews, add up the total potential score (number of the children × 10) and then record every individual's score on the board. What was the total score? What fraction of the total potential score did the book receive?
● The children could publish their review of the book on a suitable website such as www.readingmission.co.uk or www.storiesfrom theweb.org.

Differentiation
For older/more confident learners: Select a website which requires the children to write reviews as paragraphs.
For younger/less confident learners: Select a website which invites the children to write shorter reviews. Always check what has been written before publishing on the web. This will encourage the children to carry out self-assessment with real purpose!

Day and night

Objective: To write a non-narrative text using structures of different text types.
What you need: a torch, a globe, Blu-Tack®, writing materials and the ability to darken the room.

What to do

● Plop called himself a day bird as he preferred to be awake when it was light. Explain to the class that you are going to demonstrate how day changes into night.
● Use a globe and a torch in a darkened room. Explain that the torch is the Sun and that the Earth travels around the Sun in 365 days (one year). One child can hold the torch still while you demonstrates the globe travelling around the Sun. As the Earth spins around the Sun it also spins on its own axis. Now demonstrate moving around the Sun and spinning on its own axis. As the Earth turns we see the Sun for only part of the time. We call this daylight and for the rest of the time it is dark. Invite a child to stick some Blu-Tack® on the country where they live. As the Earth spins, ask the children to say whether it is day or night. Invite them to find a country on the opposite side of the globe to demonstrate that when it is day time in one country it will be night time on the other side of the globe.
● After the demonstration, invite the children to produce an information sheet with labelled diagram to explain day and night.

Differentiation
For older/more confident learners: The children can create an instruction sheet for other children to use to model day and night. Explain the use of the imperative and second person.
For younger/less confident learners: Provide the children with a diagram and labels to add in the appropriate locations.

The Duck Who Was Afraid of the Water

Imagine you are going to write your own book about a duck who was afraid of the water. Use this sheet to plan your character, setting and plot.

Name of duckling:

Describe what he/she looks like:

Describe where he/she lives:

Describe who else is in the duckling's family and what they are like:

Why is the duckling different from all the other ducklings?

Other sub-plots to include:

Character duckling meets	Water is...	Reasons:

Barn owl fact file

Use this table to plan your research about barn owls. Complete columns one, two and three before you start. When everybody is clear about the task, begin your research. Complete column four when you have found out specific facts relating to your topic search area.

What we want to find out about:	Name of research group:	Our keyword search words will be:	Information we found out:

My book review

By: _____

Title: _____

Author: _____

Illustrator: _____

My thoughts about the characters: _____

_____

_____

My thoughts about the main plot: _____

_____

_____

My thoughts about the sub plots: _____

_____

_____

My favourite part of the book: _____

_____

_____

I would change: _____

_____

_____

I would recommend this book to: _____

_____

I award this book a score of:

Assessment

Assessment advice

The Owl Who Was Afraid of the Dark is a beautifully simple and endearing book which appeals to a relatively wide age range. Its clear story structure makes it a valuable tool for teaching the children about narrative structure. Discuss the elements of narrative (such as character, setting, plot, hooks and cliff hangers) and invite the children to provide evidence of how the plot was formed, what we know about the main character both physically and relating to his personality, how the author weaved other plots into the story, and what made the book humorous. Observe the children's responses during the course of the discussion. Invite the children to challenge points of view with which they disagree and to explain their opinions.

The Duck Who Was Afraid of the Water

> **Assessment focus:** To compose and punctuate a series of sentences; to create a character and setting as an introduction to a story during supported and independent sessions (marking, feedback against agreed success criteria).
>
> **What you need:** Photocopiable page 32, writing materials, posters or images of river banks or habitats where ducks may be found and photographs of ducklings.

What to do

● Remind the children of the work carried out during the earlier writing activity when the class planned a parallel story about a duck that was afraid of the water. Explain that for their assessment you wish them to write an introduction to that story. The introduction will introduce the main character, describe what makes him/her different from the other ducklings and will describe the setting where he/she lives.

● Support the writing by displaying pictures of ducklings and river bank settings on the board. Brainstorm words to describe both. Also support the writing by referring back to the first eleven lines of *The Owl Who Was Afraid of the Dark*.

● Explain the criteria against which you are assessing the children's work – punctuation, capital letters and vocabulary choice. Actively involve the children in the assessment. Mark the work together and encourage the children to complete the checklist at the bottom of the photocopiable sheet. Provide feedback to each child on how they performed and make clear their targets for future pieces of similar writing.

The Duck Who Was Afraid of the Water

By

_____

_____

_____

_____

_____

_____

_____

My assessment checklist:

I used capital letters at the start of sentences.
I used full stops at the end of sentences.
I used capital letters for proper nouns (names).
I chose my describing words (adjectives) carefully.

My target for my next piece of writing is to: _____

_____

Signed: (Child) _____ **(Teacher)** _____